A Piggie Christmas

Howard Fine

SCHOLASTIC INC.
New York Toronto London Auckland Sydney
Mexico City New Delhi Hong Kong

Copyright © 2000 by Howard Fine. All rights reserved.
Published by Scholastic Inc., 555 Broadway, New York, NY 10012,
by arrangement with Hyperion Books for Children, an imprint of Disney
Children's Books Group, LLC. SCHOLASTIC and associated logos are
trademarks and/or registered trademarks of Scholastic Inc.

12 11 10 9 8 7 6 5 4 3 2 1   0 1 2 3 4 5 6/0

Printed in the U.S.A.   08

First Scholastic printing, November 2001

For Anne, Ken, and Katherine
–H.F.

— Contents —

The Twelve Days of Christmas

On the first day of Christmas,
my true love gave to me
a partridge in a pear tree.

On the second day of Christmas,
my true love gave to me
2 turtle doves
and a partridge in a pear tree.

On the third day of Christmas,
my true love gave to me
3 French hens,
2 turtle doves,
and a partridge in a pear tree.

On the fourth day of Christmas, my true love gave to me 4 calling birds,

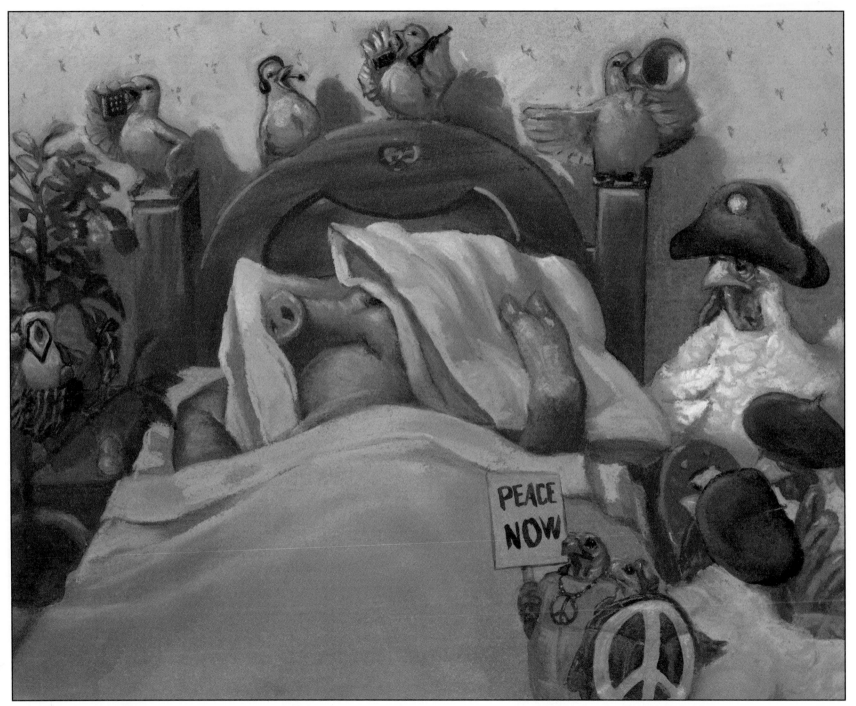

3 French hens, 2 turtle doves, and a partridge in a pear tree.

On the fifth day of Christmas, my true love gave to me **5 GOLDEN RINGS!**

4 calling birds, **3** French hens, **2** turtle doves, and a partridge in a pear tree.

On the sixth day of Christmas, my true love gave to me **6** geese a-laying,

On the seventh day of Christmas, my true love gave to me **7** swans a-swimming,

6 geese a-laying, **5** GOLDEN RINGS! **4** calling birds, **3** French hens,

2 turtle doves, and a partridge in a pear tree.

On the eighth day of Christmas, my true love gave to me **8** maids a-milking,

4 calling birds, **3** French hens, **2** turtle doves, and a partridge in

a pear tree.

On the ninth day of Christmas, my true love gave to me 9 ladies dancing,

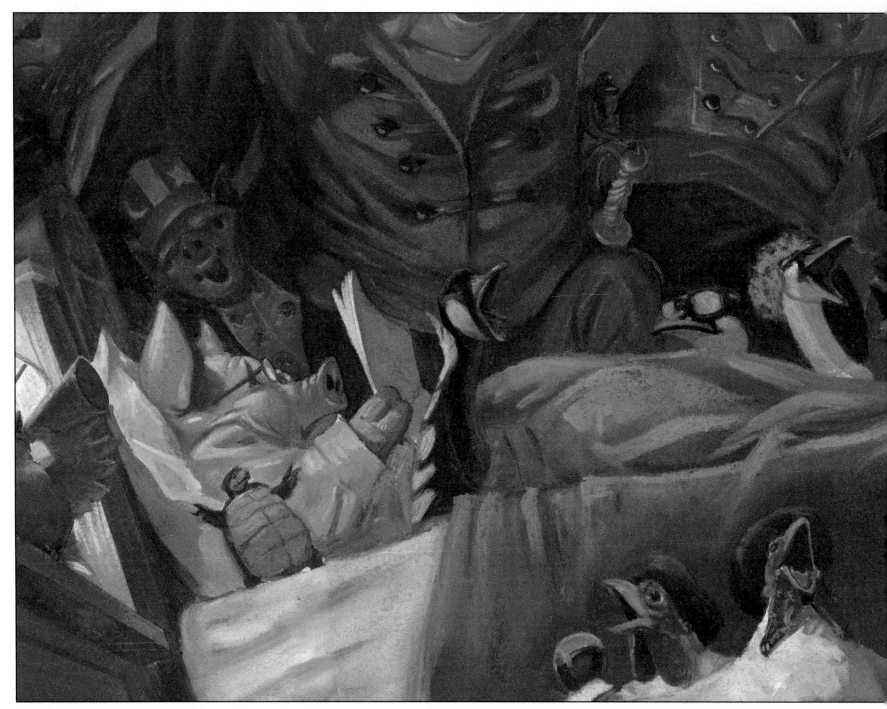

On the eleventh day of Christmas, my true love gave to me **11** pipers piping,

10 lords a-leaping, 9 ladies dancing, 8 maids a-milking, 7 swans a-swimming,

6 geese a-laying, 5 GOLDEN RINGS! 4 calling birds,

3 French hens, 2 turtle doves, and a partridge in a pear tree.

and a partridge in a pear tree.

2 turtle doves,

3 French hens,

calling birds,

On the twelfth day of Christmas, my true love gave to me **12** drummers drumming,

11 pipers piping, **10** lords a-leaping, **9** ladies dancing, **8** maids a-milking, **7** swans a-swimming, **6** geese a-laying, **5** GOLDEN RINGS

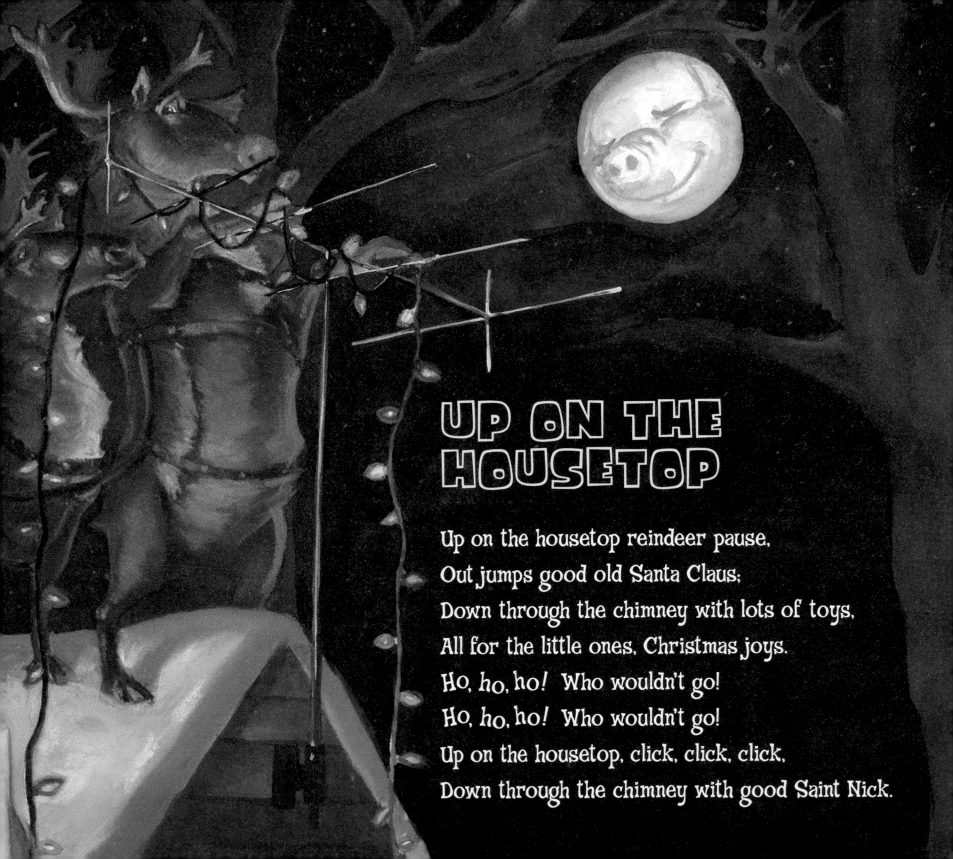

UP ON THE HOUSETOP

Up on the housetop reindeer pause,
Out jumps good old Santa Claus;
Down through the chimney with lots of toys,
All for the little ones, Christmas joys.
Ho, ho, ho! Who wouldn't go!
Ho, ho, ho! Who wouldn't go!
Up on the housetop, click, click, click,
Down through the chimney with good Saint Nick.

First comes the stocking of little Nell,

Oh, dear Santa, fill it well.

Give her a dollie that laughs and cries,

One that will open and shut her eyes.

Ho, ho, ho! Who wouldn't go!

Ho, ho, ho! Who wouldn't go!

Up on the housetop, click, click, click,

Down through the chimney with good Saint Nick.

Jingle Bells

Dashing through the snow
In a one-horse open sleigh,
O'er the fields we go,
Laughing all the way;
Bells on Bobtail ring,
Making spirits bright.
What fun it is to ride and sing
A sleighing song tonight!

Jingle bells! Jingle bells!
Jingle all the way!
Oh, what fun it is to ride
In a one-horse open sleigh!
Jingle bells! Jingle bells!
Jingle all the way!
Oh, what fun it is to ride
In a one-horse open sleigh!

Deck the Halls

Deck the halls with boughs of holly,
Fa la la la la, la la la la.
'Tis the season to be jolly,
Fa la la la la, la la la la.
Don we now our gay apparel,
Fa la la, la la la, la la la.
Troll the ancient Yuletide carol.
Fa la la la la, la la la la.

See the blazing yule before us,
Fa la la la la, la la la la.
Strike the harp and join the chorus,
Fa la la la la, la la la la.
Follow me in merry measure,
Fa la la, la la la, la la la.
While I tell of Yuletide treasure.
Fa la la la la, la la la la.

We Wish You
a Piggie Christmas

We wish you a Piggie Christmas,
We wish you a Piggie Christmas,
We wish you a Piggie Christmas,
And a Happy New Year!